Baby Horses

Lisa Idzikowski

Lerner Publications ◆ Minneapolis

For my family

Lerner Publications Company
An imprint of Lerner Publishing Group, Inc.
241 First Avenue North
Minneapolis, MN 55401 USA

For reading levels and more information, look up this title at www.lernerbooks.com.

Main body text set in Billy Infant Regular. Typeface provided by SparkType.

Photo Editor: Angel Kidd
Lerner team: Sue Marquis

Library of Congress Cataloging-in-Publication Data

Names: Idzikowski, Lisa, author.
Title: Baby horses / Lisa Idzikowski.
Description: Minneapolis : Lerner Publications, [2024] | Series: Lightning bolt books ® — horse lover's library | Includes bibliographical references and index. | Audience: Ages 6-9 | Audience: Grades 2-3 | Summary: "People love horses, and baby horses are even more irresistible. Young readers learn everything about baby horses from what their first hours of life are like to when they are fully grown"— Provided by publisher.
Identifiers: LCCN 2023034483 (print) | LCCN 2023034484 (ebook) | ISBN 9798765626047 (library binding) | ISBN 9798765628881 (paperback) | ISBN 9798765634844 (epub)
Subjects: LCSH: Foals—Juvenile literature. | Horses—Juvenile literature.
Classification: LCC SF302 .I39 2024 (print) | LCC SF302 (ebook) | DDC 636.1—dc23/eng/20230811

LC record available at https://lccn.loc.gov/2023034483
LC ebook record available at https://lccn.loc.gov/2023034484

Manufactured in the United States of America
1-1009869-51938-9/15/2023

Table of Contents

It's a Baby Horse

About an hour after being born, a baby horse tries to stand. Its legs wobble and it falls. The baby keeps trying until it takes its first steps.

Newborn horses can nurse up to six times an hour.

When the baby horse is steady, it nurses. Its mother's milk has everything the baby horse needs to stay healthy.

About four hours after being born, the baby horse can run.

A baby horse leaps in a field.

Mother and Baby

Baby horses are called foals. Adult female horses are called mares. Most mares have one foal at a time.

A pregnant mare

After giving birth, mares lick their foals to clean them off. They also snuggle their babies and smell them.

Mares protect their babies.

Day-old foals watch their mothers eat grass or hay. Soon they will try grazing.

Foals watch their mom to learn how to eat.

Mares teach their babies to look out for danger.

Horses must be aware of predators such as mountain lions and wolves.

Foals learn from their mothers when to stay calm or when to run away.

A foal runs with other horses.

A foal plays chase with its mother.

Foals also learn how to play from their mothers. If the baby bites, kicks, or plays too rough, the mare will nip or push the baby away.

Horse Homes

Many foals live on farms. Some are pets. Others grow up and help with jobs on the farm.

Some foals are wild. They live in small groups or bands of horses.

Mustangs are wild horses that live on grasslands in the western United States.

Wild horses live in all parts of the world except the Arctic and Antarctica. They live where they can find plenty of grass and fresh water.

Growing Up

Foals grow fast. At birth, they weigh about 80 to 200 pounds (36 to 91 kg). Two months later, they are three or four times that size!

Most horses are fully grown when they are about four to six years old. The biggest horses weigh up to 2,000 pounds (907 kg).

Pet horses live for about twenty-five years. Wild horses live for about fifteen years. In that time, they will run, play, and maybe even have their own babies.

Horses race through the water.

Baby Horses and You

If you were a baby horse, would you want to live on a farm or in the wild? Why?

Fun Facts

- Most foals are born at night.
- Horses have hooves, or hard foot coverings. Hooves need trimming just like fingernails.
- Grown-up male horses are called stallions.

Glossary

foal: a baby horse

grazing: eating grass

mare: an adult female horse

nip: a gentle bite

nurse: when baby animals drink their mother's milk

predator: an animal that hunts and eats other animals for food

weigh: to find out how heavy something is

Learn More

Britannica Kids: Horse
https://kids.britannica.com/kids/article/horse/353265

Kiddle: Horse Facts for Kids
https://kids.kiddle.co/Horse

Krenn, Cara. *Wild Horses*. Minneapolis: Lerner Publications, 2025.

Pang, Ursula. *Horse Farms*. New York: PowerKids, 2023.

Rathburn, Betsy. *Baby Horses*. Minneapolis: Bellwether Media, 2022.

Index

Photo Acknowledgments

image credits: oxygen/Getty Images, p. 4; George Pachantouris/Getty Images, p. 5; Anna-av/Getty Images, pp. 6, 20; Noppawat Tom Charoensinphon/Getty Images, p. 10; John Conrad/Getty Images, p. 11; Gigja Einarsdottir/Getty Images, p. 12; happyborder/Getty Images, p. 14; alder7/Getty Images, p. 16; mgstudyo/Getty Images, p. 19; Jolanda Aalbers/Shutterstock, p. 7; pfluegler-photo/Shutterstock, p. 8; Alberto Duran Photography/Shutterstock, p. 9; Coryn/Shutterstock, p. 13; Ronnie Howard/Shutterstock, pp. 15, 20; Susanna K/Shutterstock, p. 17; Azahara Perez/Shutterstock, p. 18.

Cover photo: mari_art/Getty Images.